# Modern Discoveries
# in Archaeology

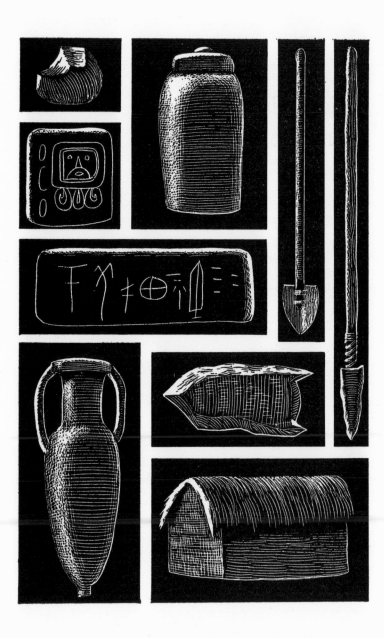

# Modern Discoveries in Archaeology

*By Robert C. Suggs*

*Illustrated by Leonard Everett Fisher*

THOMAS Y. CROWELL COMPANY / NEW YORK

To Wayne

*'E tama 'a'u'!*
*'Ua mate ho'i te tai kakiu, 'a tuha'e!*
*Tiohi anaiho i te'a'e tihemai ne'i!*

# Contents

# List of Full-Page Illustrations

# INTRODUCTION

"ARCHAEOLOGY" to most people means the opening of King Tutankhamen's tomb by Howard Carter, Sir Leonard Woolley digging at Ur, Heinrich von Schliemann probing the ruins of Troy or any of a number of startling and colorful discoveries in the exciting history of archaeological explorations. The general public opinion seems to be that the great discoveries of archaeology have been made in the past; one has to go back twenty or thirty years or more to find a discovery that is reasonably well known to the average person.

This oversight on the part of the public is probably due, at least in part, to the fact that archaeological news is forced to compete for newspaper space these days with news of earth-shaking importance. The great events of war, international politics, the atom bomb and the furious and exciting "race for space" have combined to limit seriously the coverage that archaeologists can expect for their discoveries. It is not exaggerating to say that if King Tutankhamen's tomb were to be found today, it would receive no more than a very small percentage of the publicity that heralded its discovery in 1922; the editors would simply have to make room for other news of at least equal importance.

In spite of this restriction on the amount of information on archaeology that reaches the public, there has certainly been no curtailment of archaeological research. Moreover, there are many more archaeologists today, in universities and museums or conducting archaeological explorations in the field, than there were in the golden days of the late 1800's and early 1900's, when so many of the currently well-known discoveries were made. Not only are there more archaeologists, but the aims and scope of archaeology have changed considerably since the days of Woolley and Evans.

For example, the great discoveries and advances in archaeology during recent years have not taken place among the temples and tombs of Egypt, the white-columned ruins of ancient Rome or the sun-baked mounds of ruined cities in the Near East. Much of the most important archaeology has been done in areas that until recently were often not considered worth the effort of archaeological exploration. It is only since 1926 that we have had any knowledge about the past of the American Indian in many parts of North America, and explorations have paid handsome dividends in knowledge of South American Indian archaeology. Africa, the Dark Continent, has only now been partially illuminated archaeologically to show an unexpected wealth of archaeological resources covering a huge span of years. The jungles of Southeast Asia and the islands of the Pacific Ocean are also beginning to yield a fascinating tale of human history as archaeologists continue to probe these "unexplored" areas of the archaeological map. Furthermore, archaeology has not been content to expand over the land surface, but has now dipped beneath the surface of the sea.

In addition to this considerable geographical expansion of archaeological activity, there has been great progress made in actual archaeological methods and techniques enabling the archaeologists to wring more information out of an excavated site than they ever have in the past.

Radiocarbon dating, which is discussed in the first chapter, has enabled us to measure accurately the age of archaeological remains over tens of thousands of years old, where before we could only guess at the age of much that was found. Aerial photography techniques developed for military reconnaissance have shown buried archaeological sites which were often not visible to a person on the surface of the ground. Recovering and identifying tiny grains of pollen from the earth of archaeological sites has made possible the reconstruction of climate and vegetation of ancient times. Chemical tests have been developed that will demonstrate the presence of burials in a site even when the skeletons have completely decayed.

Archaeologists have worked out many new techniques of their own for use in their investigations. A method known as artifact seriation now enables us to determine when and for how long archaeological sites were inhabited, on the basis of analysis of a sample of pottery or other tools collected from its surface. The use of heavy excavating machinery for rapid excavation has been tried, and machines have even been used to sift earth and pick up potsherds from the surface.

These advances unfortunately are not so well known as those that occurred in the past, received great acclaim and have had time to filter into grammar and high school texts and become part of the education of a generation or two of youngsters. But many of the more recent discoveries are fully as important as those which have become so famous through the years in terms of the amount that they have taught us about man's past. Indeed, they may be more important.

This book is devoted to a discussion of a number of these great archaeological discoveries of the present. By "present" is meant the years since World War II, with the exception of one particularly important and quite neglected discovery stemming from the 1920's which I felt deserved inclusion. Now, selecting the "great" archaeological discoveries that have occurred recently is by no means an easy task, as there have been many, many discoveries, each important in one

4

way or another for greater or lesser numbers of archaeologists. If one looks at the New World alone, the accounts of archaeological discoveries of importance might fill a book several times this size.

If this consideration is extended to cover the archaeological discoveries of the entire world, then selection of the important discoveries becomes even more difficult. For what is important for an American-trained archaeologist like myself is often not important at all for an equally competent Chinese archaeologist, let us say, because our areas of interest and specialization have relatively little overlap. Therefore, he would have relatively little interest in the discovery of an ancient Indian spear point in the bones of a mastodon in Arizona, for example, whereas such a discovery would be most interesting to me.

For these reasons, I have selected for inclusion in this book the discoveries that seem to me to have had the most significance for the world as a whole, in terms of expanding our knowledge about the important periods of human history in the major continents.

The first discovery to be discussed in this book is perhaps one of the most significant of all, for our thinking about the age of mankind has been changed by it considerably, yet it was made as a result of very modern research in a scientific field that is as far from archaeology as imaginable.

# 1/ CLOCK OF THE AGES

HAVE YOU EVER held an ancient Indian arrowhead in your hand and wondered: How old is it? How many years ago did this piece of chipped flint whistle through the air on the tip of a feathered arrow, seeking the heart of an enemy, a white-tailed deer or a mountain lion? When I was very young my grandfather brought me a stone tomahawk that he had found in his garden. I spent many hours examining that beautifully polished piece of stone with its finely ground edge, wondering about just those questions. But no one could give me the answers I wanted.

Archaeologists were often led to ask the same questions because they sometimes had no way whatever of knowing the ages of the ancient camps, villages and tombs that they excavated. In Egypt, hieroglyphic inscriptions often told archaeologists the ages of tombs and monuments. The inscriptions would say that the monument in question had been built during the reign of king so-and-so. As we had the Egyptians' own written lists of all their kings and the lengths of each king's reign we could figure out the age of the monument. The same method of dating was used to find

7

the age of Greek and Roman ruins. Their historians had obligingly left us histories with which it was rather simple to date their temples and palaces. In the Holy Land, dates of some ruined cities could often be deduced from information found in the Bible. Old Stone Age sites were often dated on the basis of the geological deposits in which they were found. If we knew that site X had been found in a particular layer of earth deposited by the fourth glacier of the Pleistocene Ice Age, then we could say that site X was as old as the fourth glacier, but the exact age of the fourth glacier could not be exactly known.

Around the Mediterranean Sea, where well-known Egyptian, Greek and Roman objects had been carried by ancient trading ships and caravans, it was possible to find out the age of an unknown site if one could turn up a Roman or Greek coin or a piece of Egyptian pottery the date of which had already been determined in Rome, Greece or Egypt.

In America, however, it was very difficult for

archaeologists to find the age of Indian remains. Temple mounds, burial mounds, villages, pueblos and shell heaps were excavated all over the United States. In many parts of this country, archaeologists had determined which of the villages, burial mounds, and camp sites were the oldest, which were the youngest and which were of medium age. Only where they found the tools and ornaments of the early American colonists mixed with Indian tools, indicating that the Indians had met the whites, could they know how many years ago the camp or village had been inhabited.

Now, however, thanks to one of the most momentous discoveries in the history of archaeology, we can tell the age of almost anything that an archaeologist finds. We can know how many years have elapsed since the ashes of an Old Stone Age campfire grew cold. And we can tell how long it has been since the brown callused feet of Indians trod the earth of an ancient village discovered near what is now New York City.

Strangely enough, this discovery was not made in the jungles of Yucatan, nor in the midst of a sandswept Egyptian temple, nor by the side of a weatherbeaten Pueblo cliff dwelling in Colorado. It was not even made by an archaeologist.

The discovery that has helped us turn back the

clock of ages was made by Dr. Willard Libby, a nuclear chemist, in the University of Chicago Institute for Nuclear Studies. More surprising is the fact that this discovery was an outgrowth of the tremendous research project that led to our first atomic bomb.

What does the atomic bomb research have to do with the age of ancient cities? The answer to that question makes a fascinating story.

After World War II, Dr. Libby was conducting research on a radioactive element called Carbon 14. This element had been discovered some years before, but little work had ever been done on it, and Dr. Libby was doing a complete job of tracking it down. He wanted to know how it was formed, where it could be found in abundance and what function it served, if any. It was believed that atomic bombs could produce this element, but before this could be known, more had to be known about C 14 (the chemists' abbreviation for Carbon 14).

Carbon 14 is formed in dizzy heights of our upper atmosphere. Here streams of electromagnetic energy particles called cosmic rays bombard the molecules of air. This bombardment of tiny particles succeeds in knocking loose neutrons (small uncharged particles in the nucleus of an atom) from the molecules of air. A neutron set free in this fashion wanders about, often

10

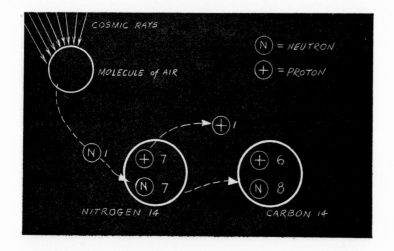

entering an atom of Nitrogen 14 (N 14), another very
common element in the atmosphere. Nitrogen 14 is so
called because it has seven neutrons and seven protons
(positively charged particles) in its nucleus. When a
wandering neutron enters, however, one of the protons
is ejected and replaced by the neutron, transforming
the atom of nitrogen into an atom of Carbon 14 with
six protons and eight neutrons.

The Carbon 14 diffuses in the atmosphere and
unites with oxygen to form carbon dioxide. With the
aid of sunlight, plants use carbon dioxide to produce
their food. Human beings and probably almost all
land animals also need a very small amount of carbon
dioxide in the air that they breathe: it stimulates
breathing. We also eat both plants and animals con-

**11**

taining C 14, thereby getting additional amounts of it.

Thus, Dr. Libby found that C 14 gets into all plants and animals. But the amount is very small: according to his calculations there is one lonely C 14 atom for every trillion atoms of other types in living things. If all the C 14 atoms in the world were put together, he calculated that their total weight would be only about seventy-nine tons—the size of a bombing plane!

Dr. Libby next wanted to find a source of C 14 so that he could conduct experiments with it to see how it behaved under various conditions. He found it easiest to obtain in the foul-smelling gas from sewage, called methane. From a sample of sewage obtained in Baltimore, he worked up a quantity of C 14 for his research.

The C 14 atom was found to be very unstable because of its extra neutron. Something was seriously out of balance in the atom and it kept trying to throw off a chunk of itself, to get things in balance again.

Finally, an electron (a negatively charged particle) was expelled from the nucleus, and one of the neutrons of the C 14 nucleus changed to a proton, thus giving the atom 7 neutrons and 7 protons again, changing it back into N 14. Dr. Libby found that C 14 was changing to nitrogen at a steady rate. But as long as the plant or animal was alive, the C 14 that changed to nitrogen was replaced by new C 14 in the air, so that the amount in the plant or animal always remained constant.

When a plant or animal died, however, no new C 14 would get into the dead tissues, and the C 14 would continue changing to nitrogen until none was left. Dr. Libby predicted that it would take 5,568 years for the C 14 in anything to reduce itself by one-half. He had to have some way to check his predictions, however, and so he thought: Where would it be possible to obtain some ancient wood, charcoal or fiber whose age was already known? The archaeologists, of course! They could supply him with wood from well-dated archaeological excavations all over the world. He could test for the amount of C 14 in the plant material, and compare his results with the amount his predictions told him should be there, on the basis of their known age.

If the tests for C 14 in each of the wood samples agreed with his predictions, then he would know that his theories about C 14 were correct. It would then be possible to use the C 14 tests to find the age of any archaeological site in the world.

The samples for the tests were collected: a piece of the door from King Snefru's pyramid tomb in Egypt, built in 2690 B.C., a fragment of a funeral boat used in the funeral of Senusret III 3,800 years ago, and a bit of a mummy case made in the Ptolemaic period in Egypt (about 300 B.C.). Samples of wood were also taken from the rings of ancient sequoia trees that had lived in California a thousand years before the birth of Christ. One such sample was taken from the heart of a three-thousand-year-old giant that had lived until 1874, when it fell.

These samples were tested, and at first the results seemed only fair: the dates arrived at by the C 14 tests were a few hundred years away from the known dates. Gradually, Dr. Libby refined his techniques, and soon the results were much closer to the known dates. Within a short time, the C 14 test technique was worked out so that it was quite accurate. A sample of wood would be subjected to various chemical processes to remove the carbon, containing C 14.

14

The carbon was then placed in a radiation counter, a sensitive instrument with which the number of electrons given off by the C 14 could be counted, and the amount of change from C 14 to N 14 in the sample could be determined. By counting the number of electrons emitted by the sample, which had been carefully measured, it was possible to tell how much C 14 remained in the carbon. If the radiation counter showed electrons being emitted rapidly, the sample obviously contained a sizable amount of C 14 and therefore was relatively new. If, on the other hand, only a small number of electrons were emitted, there was only a small amount of C 14 left in the sample, which was therefore relatively old.

From exact measurements of the radioactivity remaining in the carbon sample it was possible to calculate the number of years that had gone by since the material in the sample had been part of a living plant. If, for example, only half of the normal amount of the element was present, then the scientist would know that the sample was 5,568 years old. Because of equipment adjustments, and various kinds of disturbances, the readings never came out exactly to any given year. All dates were given with a "margin of error" to account for lack of precision. Sometimes this would be small, say, fifty years or so. On very old specimens the margin of error might be as large as a thousand years or more. But even this error is still much, much better than guessing.

Archaeologists realized the importance of Dr. Libby's work immediately and he was besieged by people offering samples for him to test. Very wisely, only the most important samples were chosen for testing at first and the results were amazing. In New York State, the remains of ancient Indians known as the Archaic People had been thought to be about twenty-five hundred years old, at most. Researchers tested samples from Archaic campfires from several sites. The age: *3500 years* B.C.

For many years experts had disagreed over the way that the ancient Mayan calendar should be fitted into our calendar. Two major theories had been presented on this subject but there had never been any way of checking the correctness of either. Then Dr. Libby's C 14 tests were developed and the opportunity was finally there. In the huge ancient Mayan city of Tikal, deep in the Guatemalan rain forests, archaeologists had found many temples and buildings with doorways capped by heavy wooden lintels of sapodilla wood, a common wood in the Mayan region that has amazing resistance to age and decay. Carved on the lintels, in strange Mayan hieroglyphs, were the dates at which the buildings had been built. Using samples of wood taken from these dated door lintels and

wooden roof beams inside the buildings, the archaeologists proceeded to test the theories developed by various scholars for relating the Christian calendar dates to the Mayan calendar dates.

Two major theories existed: according to one, the Mayan calendar date "9.15.10.0.0" represented A.D. 481 of the Christian calendar. The other held, however, that "9.15.10.0.0" actually represented A.D. 741. Although first tests seemed to indicate that the first theory was correct, a large number of tests performed with great care on many samples proved conclusively that "9.15.10.0.0" of the Mayans was actually A.D. 741.

Now archaeologists can visit a Mayan site, copy the dates from one of the vine-covered monuments or a broken-down temple door, and with a little calculation translate the Mayan date to a figure that will tell approximately how many years ago the monument was built or the temple constructed.

Before Libby's method was introduced, sites of the Palaeolithic or Old Stone Age in Europe were datable, as we have mentioned, only by reference to glacial deposits.

Now, however, dates were obtained from campfires in many of the ancient caves of Europe. These dates immediately showed that many of the scientists' estimates had been too distant, while others were too recent. The Magdalenian reindeer hunters, for example, were previously thought to have existed about twenty-five thousand years ago, but are now known to have lived about fifteen thousand years ago.

In the islands of the Pacific, C 14 has helped with the problem of dating immeasurably. Those of us who have been tracing the origins of the Polynesian people have had much occasion to give thanks for Dr. Libby's discoveries. C 14 tests have helped us to see that many of the Polynesian islands were inhabited over one thousand years earlier than anyone had thought, while the islands in the Western Pacific appear to have been inhabited even earlier, at a time two thousand years or so before Christ.

The discovery of the C 14 dating technique, then, was one of the greatest discoveries of archaeology. It has brought about a revolution in our views on the age of man's habitation in many parts of the globe. Without it we would still be unsatisfactorily dating archaeological remains by reference to geological deposits or by "educated" guesses.

At present, C 14 dating has proven to be of value for artifacts of less than 70,000 years old. Now 70,000 years is a very large period of time, but man and his fossil ancestors have roamed this earth for a much longer time than that—a period over ten times longer, or about 750,000 years. Techniques similar to the C 14 method, but using other radioactive elements, have been developed for dating archaeological materials of these greater ages.

The reader will want to know what our ancestors of that time looked like, and how they lived. These questions will be answered in the next chapter, which deals with one of the most important early-man finds to be made in years—a discovery made in the wild wastelands of East Africa in 1959.

# 2/ THE FIRST TOOLMAKER

IN MANY MUSEUMS, the chipped stone tools of the Old Stone Age men can be seen, arranged in neat rows and labeled so that the visitor may know where they were found. Some of these tools are simply crude stone flakes, with a sharpened edge or a rounded end, designed to serve as a knife or a scraper. Other, more famous tools are what the archaeologist calls "hand axes"—big leaf-shaped stone tools with sharp points, blunt ends and keen edges. Such tools are very old— some of them dating back to 500,000 years ago, and one might therefore think that they are scarce.

There is, however, a place where one can find hundreds of thousands of such tools, *and some even older*, just lying around on the surface of the ground, like ordinary stones! It might appear a very tall tale, for such an archaeologist's paradise seems too good to be true. But there is just such a place; and it is the setting for this story of the discovery of the first toolmaker.

Perhaps this may not seem like such an important thing to discover, but just think where we would be today without tools. Not one object around us could exist without complicated tools of all varieties. Human beings are the only animals on the face of the earth who make and use tools, and it is this ability that has enabled us to rise so high above our animal relatives. So the first toolmakers were actually extremely important, for they started the chain of inventions and technological developments that has been unbroken right up to today.

But to get back to this archaeologists' paradise, before you get your knapsacks packed and try to buy a train ticket, let me tell you that it is located far away from the United States, in a strange place called Olduvai Gorge in Tanganyika, East Africa, an isolated, uninhabited area of the world. No people live in this dry, rocky area today, and only lions, rhinos and some smaller game wander over the rocky ground amid the scrubs and bushes. Once, however, in the Ice Age, tens of thousands of years ago, this valley was a huge lake bed, and men of the Old Stone Age made their camps on the shores of the lake while they hunted game, fished, and gathered roots and berries.

When these ancient hunters left, their camps were littered with broken stone tools and the bones of animals they had killed and eaten. Gradually the camps were covered by earth, washed down into the lake from the surrounding mountains, and more men came to make camp on the new land surface thus formed. Layer after layer of earth built up in the lake bed

through the centuries as men came and went. Finally, when the Ice Age was over, the lake went dry. A river began to flow through the lake bed, cutting down into the accumulated layers of earth in which the Stone Age camps were buried. Soon a deep gorge was formed, winding through the valley floor like a miniature Grand Canyon. It displayed in its steep, weathered sides the layers of earth which hold the records of hundreds of thousands of years of human history.

Olduvai Gorge is the best Old Stone Age site in the world. In the deepest layers, exposed at the very base of the gorge, are found the earliest implements ever made by human hands, the crude tools that mark man's first attempt at manufacturing an object that would do a job better than his bare hands.

These crude implements are called "pebble tools" by archaeologists, because they are made from rounded pebbles, about the size of a potato, from the end of which a few chips have been knocked off to make a crude cutting edge and point. The edges of the pebble tools are worn smooth as if by long use, as are the edges of the rough stone flakes found with them. Archaeologists have surmised that the makers of these tools used them to butcher animals, the bones of which are found in great numbers with the pebble tools.

By studying and testing these animal bones and the soils in the early beds, scientists have been able to show that these early pebble tools were made some 1,500,000 years ago. Think of it—stone implements one and one-half million years old, appearing today in almost as good condition as when their makers discarded them by a huge African lake so long ago!

Until a very short time ago the identity of the makers of the pebble tools remained a dark secret, because not a scrap of human bone had been found in the pebble tool beds. But now that is no longer the case, thanks to a most exciting discovery.

In 1959 a famous British archaeologist, Dr. L. S. B. Leakey, made the hot, tiring trip over almost non-existent trails to visit Olduvai Gorge as he had done many times before. Dr. Leakey wished to add to his collections of stone implements from the "layer-cake" walls of the gorge and see if any new implements or fossil animals had been washed out of the steep gorge sides. Dr. Leakey was accompanied by his wife, also an accomplished archaeologist, who had assisted him in all of his work on the Old Stone Age men of Africa. With the aid of trained native assistants, the two archaeologists began a systematic search of the floor of the long, winding gorge, picking over the stone axes and flakes that littered the earth under foot, and scaling the steep sides of the gorge to pluck out specimens still held in the layers of earth exposed there.

The collecting was going along quite well when Mrs. Leakey noticed a bit of bright ivory-colored substance in the reddish earth at her feet. She picked it up and saw to her amazement a large but very human-like tooth. Her trained archaeologist's eye told her that this was not the tooth of any ordinary human, however, for not only was it very large but it was completely fossilized. Nevertheless, the pattern of wrinkles and bumps on the crown of the tooth were very much like those on human teeth. Where had the tooth come from? And if the tooth had appeared, could the skull be far behind? Mrs. Leakey looked up the side of the gorge. Had it washed down from there?

Soon she was scrambling up the slope searching the pebble-tool beds for the skeleton, hoping that it had not been smashed or washed away and hidden in some crevice of the gorge beneath tons of earth.

Then she saw a bit of bone protruding from the ground. She knelt and brushed away the coarse earth, and an unexpected sight emerged: the side of a massive skull, like that of a human being in many ways but also different in many features. Dr. Leakey and his assistants were soon at her side; they began to work in earnest. Using fine brushes and dental tools, they stripped away the dust of ages from the base of the rugged skull, which was reposing, upside down, in the pebble-tool bed. The skull had lain there ever since a day some 1,500,000 years ago when its owner had lain down to die among the bones of the animals he had hunted and the crude tools that he had used.

Here was the answer to the scientists' queries about the identity of the pebble-tool makers! The Leakeys excavated the whole area around the spot where the

skull had appeared and found that it had evidently
been a camp site. Stone tools were particularly numerous, as were bones of many small animals: lizards,
snakes and four-footed beasts that the possessor of
the skull had once feasted upon. Evidently, this early
man had died and been abandoned without burial by
his comrades in their camp.

As soon as Dr. Leakey returned to his laboratory
with the treasured skull carefully packed to protect it
from any possible damage, he began the long process
of cleaning and examining his find, and then an even
more surprising fact appeared. The skull, with its
huge teeth, massive brow ridges and small brain

cavity, did not represent a new variety of fossil man. Rather, it was almost identical with fossils called Australopithecinae that had been found in South Africa since the 1920's. These fossils had been termed "apeman," for they displayed in their bones many characteristics of the apes, but their leg and pelvic bones showed that they had walked upright and their hands were not like those of apes but like ours. Because they seemed to represent a creature about halfway between man and ape, their discoverer, Dr. Raymond Dart, an Australian anatomist, had identified them as being the "missing link."

In all the previous South African archaeological excavations, however, there had never been one stone tool found with these fossil apemen, and many scientists concluded that they were so primitive they were unable to make tools. Dr. Dart claimed that they had made tools of bone and stone, but few believed him, for the tools he displayed had never been found in close association with an Australopithecus fossil.

Now, however, Dr. Dart was shown to be correct, and the world knew the identity of the first inquisitive near-humans who decided to better their lot three-quarters of a million years ago. By making stone implements, they made their difficult hand-to-mouth existence easier. If we look at the great scientific developments of the present—globe-circling satellites, atom-powered ships, television, radio and magic computers, we can be more than a little proud of the long road that the human race has traveled since the days of the Australopithecus fossils and their pebble tools. But without the efforts of these first craftsmen, squatting in the mud of an African beach amid the bloody remains of their meals, we would never have arrived at our present level of scientific development. It was they who took the first step, they who made the first tools, and if we probe the background of any of the most advanced wonders of science far enough into the past, we always return to that African beach and the talented apemen that Dr. and Mrs. Leakey have identified for us as the first toolmakers.

# 3/ STONE AGE DISASTER

SEVERAL HUNDRED THOUSAND years later the Australopithecus man apes were no longer seen in Africa, and new types of fossil men trod the water holes and lake beds that the man apes had once frequented. From Africa, man's ancestors gradually spread over the globe, and as the process of human evolution brought about changes in their appearance, so their culture also changed and improved.

For the next story of discovery we will jump ahead in time more than 1,400,000 years and move our focus to Northern Iraq to consider a discovery of a kind of human ancestor that was much different in physical form and way of life from Australopithecus man apes of Africa.

Northern Iraq is a wild country of jagged snow-capped peaks towering above grassy, tree-dotted slopes, and deep valleys, cut by rivers that turn to raging torrents in the spring thaws. The people of this region are proud warrior-herdsmen called Kurds. These tanned mountaineers, dressed in baggy pants and turbans, are seldom seen without the rifles and cartridge belts that are to them an important part of

31

a man's normal clothing. They need their rifles for self-defense, for they are divided into tribes which are almost continually at war with each other, and raids are common even today. Herding their goats and sheep with the aid of great savage mastiffs with smooth coats and cropped ears, the Kurds live what might appear to us an unsettled existence, roaming the cool mountains during the summer, and wintering in small valley villages.

This region of such beauty and danger is also one of the most archaeologically interesting in the Near East, for in the river valleys and on the foothills are low mounds studded with crumbling walls, and covered with the broken fragments of ancient pottery jars, marking the sites of villages and towns of thousands of years ago. In many caves formed in the rocky mountainsides are the remains of still older men: those who lived during the Old Stone Age, long before villages and towns were ever dreamed of. They hunted the huge elephantlike mastodons and buffalo that lived on the fringes of the Ice Age glaciers not far to the north.

It was the possibility of finding such Old Stone Age caves that lured a young American archaeologist, Dr. Ralph Solecki, into this region in 1950. Dr. Solecki spent a long time roaming the mountains with Kurdish guides, going from one cave to another, digging "test

pits" in the cave floors to see what things might be hidden beneath and examining the ground just outside the cave mouths for any stone tools that might have washed out of the caves. Finally he arrived at the Big Cave of Shanidar, a cave about eighty feet high and three hundred feet deep, high in the mountains, near the Zab River. As it was summer, the cave was being lived in by Kurds, sheltering there from the withering heat with their goats, mastiffs and chickens. On the slope outside the cave mouth Dr. Solecki found many chipped flint tools of Stone Age type; they were washing out of the earth. The Kurds were striking these ancient flint fragments on pieces of steel to produce sparks for their tobacco pipes and their fires.

The large number of stone tools outside the cave gave good promise of rich digging inside, so Dr. Solecki addressed himself to the Kurds: would they let him dig? After a little discussion with the headman of the group, the permission was granted. But the Kurds would not move the pens they had built for their goats, so the excavations had to be made in the center of the cave floor whether it was suitable or not. The test pit was begun with the aid of the Kurds. It was a long narrow trench which would facilitate study of a cross-section of the layers of the cave floor. These untrained archaeological helpers had to be watched closely lest they make a mistake that would result in the destruction of a piece of archaeological evidence.

Just below the surface of Shanidar Cave was a thin layer of earth about one and a half feet deep in which were found broken pottery beads and stone tools of the Neolithic or *New* Stone Age Period, a time when men lived in villages, raised grain and animals and made pottery. Below this layer was another, much thicker layer of earth, in which very different artifacts appeared beneath the spades and trowels of Solecki's rifle-toting part-time archaeologists. This layer had been formed just before the start of the New Stone Age: the stone knives, spear points and scraping tools told the archaeologist that these tools dated from twelve thousand years ago.

In a few feet of digging, the Kurdish diggers had already spanned a tremendous period of time. But digging did not cease at that level, for beneath it was another layer, containing the carefully chipped flint blades, engraving tools, spear points and scrapers of the Old Stone Age men of some twenty-nine thousand to thirty-four thousand years ago. The workmen had not yet reached the rock bottom of the big cave, for there was still another layer beneath, consisting of a deep deposit of earth that was stained with ashes and charcoal and streaked with the remains of ancient fires. This rested on the rock of the original cave floor.

In this layer were boulders so huge that Dr. Solecki had to break them with skillfully placed charges of dynamite that sent the Kurdish chickens skyrocketing through the cave mouth in a burst of feathers and squawks, while the big dogs retreated to safety, their tails between their legs. The boulders had evidently broken from the cave ceiling in an earthquake many thousands of years before and fallen to the floor. Earthquakes in this region are quite common even today, and one occurred while Dr. Solecki was deep in the test pit, directing his native helpers at close range. Fortunately, the deep excavation did not cave in—although the tremors shook loose small rocks and earth from the pit sides.

In this lowest level of Shanidar some interesting Stone Age tools appeared: big triangular spear points, small hand axes, stone scrapers and knives. To the excited archaeologist they meant one thing: Shanidar Cave had been inhabited by Neanderthal Man! These particular tools were clues to the presence of those

short, massive men of the last glacial period whose low-browed, broad faces and receding jaws have become well known to science students the world over.

These ancient hunters had first moved into Shanidar some seventy thousand years before and made it their home for thousands of years through the cruel winters and short summers of the last great advance of the glacial ice. The thickness of the deposit of earth with its discarded stone tools and campfires showed that the Neanderthal men had visited Shanidar's shelter often and stayed long.

For a time, it appeared that only the broken or discarded stone tools remained of the stoop-shouldered Old Stone Age tenants. Then, one day, a workman called for Solecki to come and see what had been found. There, about twenty-eight feet below the surface of the big cave, a skeleton had come to light. A Neanderthal skeleton? The prospect was terribly exciting to the American archaeologist, for Neanderthal skeletons are by no means common, especially in Iraq. The tedious job of clearing the skeleton began; immediately excitement grew: clearly, it was not an adult skeleton at all, but that of a young child. Not one Neanderthal child of this age had ever been unearthed before. This would answer the question of whether the unusual features of the adult Neanderthal skull and skeleton developed in early childhood or later. It turned out that these features did begin to develop in childhood.

But the scientific world had to wait until Dr. Solecki had visited his remarkable cave several more times before the strange and tragic story of Shanidar's Neanderthal inhabitants became clear.

On a later visit to the cave Solecki found that the earthquake which had cluttered up the thick Neanderthal level of the cave with boulders about sixty thousand years ago had not occurred when the cave was empty. Down among the massive chunks of limestone, *skeletons of crushed Neanderthal victims of that catastrophe began to appear.* Solecki reconstructed the story in this way: A group of Neanderthals had been lounging about the cave, probably in the evening or during inclement weather; otherwise they would more likely have been outside, out of the danger zone. Perhaps they were talking of the hunting that day or gossiping about the everyday quarrels and jokes that were certainly as important in their way of life as in ours. At the same time, they were performing the usual jobs that were necessary: making stone tools, getting their spears and hunting tackle ready, fixing skins for clothing.

Suddenly the earth trembled and dust sifted from cracks in the cave ceiling. They had started for the mouth of the cave yards away when a vicious shock

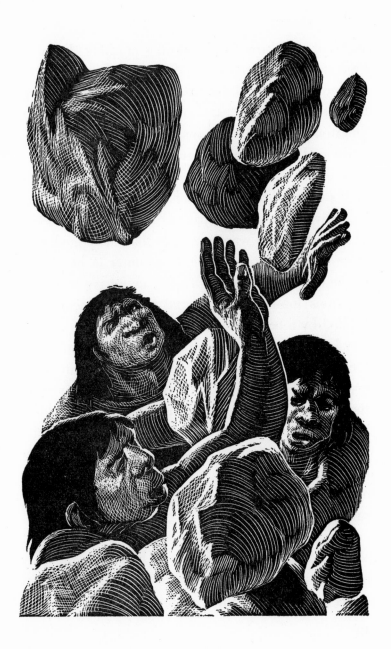

struck it and brought the ceiling crashing down on their heads. Of those who made it safely to the door we know nothing. They, of course, left without a trace. Only the unfortunates smashed beneath the fallen limestone cave ceiling remained to tell us the story of the end of a Stone Age family.

One of these unlucky individuals had already had a very unusual life, as Dr. Solecki and his colleagues found when they reconstructed his crushed skeleton. This Neanderthal was an elderly man of rugged physique who had probably been a hunter in his youth. In the course of a hunting trip he may have sustained a serious injury—he appeared to have been badly mauled by a bear or some other wild animal. The injury left permanent scars on his head and resulted in the loss of his right arm at the elbow. The arm, however, had obviously not been completely removed by the bear but had been neatly *amputated* at the elbow by a talented fellow Neanderthal. Primitive peoples are often good at minor surgery, but no one had ever suspected that Stone Age men could perform major operations. This is the earliest known example of surgery in ancient man.

The loss of an arm did not stop this stalwart Neanderthal. He found a way to be of use and may have become a flint worker, holding the stone flakes in his hand and the antler chipping tools in his teeth.

His upper front teeth were forced out to the sides of his mouth by the pressure of holding this tool so tightly. He was probably working diligently away at his stone tools at the fateful hour when the earth tremor signaled the end of his hard life.

Besides the amputee's skeleton, five others were discovered sprawled beneath the limestone chunks, five who had joined him in death. Some were probably related to him, for it is believed that Neanderthals traveled in family groups. So we now have seven Neanderthal skeletons from the Shanidar Cave, if we include the child found early in 1950—more skeletons than have been recovered from any other Neanderthal site in the world. Furthermore, we know that all of these people lived at exactly the same time and died at the same time. In addition, the six adults may have been members of the same or related families, an important point for scientists, who can now see if related Neanderthal men were more or less alike than closely related modern people, and determine what body features displayed this close family relationship most clearly.

Thus a horrible tragedy, dated by Carbon 14 as having occurred seventy thousand years ago in the Old Stone Age, has been a blessing for modern archaeology.

# 4/  EARLY BISON HUNTERS
# OF THE NEW WORLD

UP TO NOW we have been dealing with discoveries relating to the ancient inhabitants of the Old World —Africa and Asia—but we now will discuss some of the early men of the New World—the descendants of the *first* discoverers of America, who entered this continent over land and ice bridges from Asia. While the human race passed through hundreds of thousands of years of physical and cultural evolution in the Old World, the continents that would one day be called North and South America were inhabited only by lower animals. But one day men from Eastern Asia set out toward the rising sun and discovered the vast continent to the east.

In 1926, a group of scientists from the Colorado Museum were digging through layers of clay and gravel near the banks of the Cimarron River, not far from the little town of Folsom, New Mexico. These men were palaeontologists, that is, they were scientists studying ancient forms of animal and plant life. They were looking for skeletons of a particular kind of animal that had been discovered in that area: an unusual

43

type of bison that thousands of years ago had roamed what is now New Mexico. These ancient bison, known to the scientists as Bison taylorii, were different from the present-day bison seen on the American plains, and it was believed they had become extinct centuries before either Indian or white man had set foot on the North American continent.

Beneath the surface of the dry New Mexico soil the diggers struck pay dirt. Buried by fourteen feet of earth accumulated by erosion through the long years were complete bison skeletons of the type for which they were searching. The bison were lying where they had died or been killed in ages past.

The palaeontologists began to uncover carefully the bones of the big long-horned animals. Working slowly and patiently, with an assortment of brushes, whisk brooms, trowels and scraping tools, they removed the earth surrounding the bones, and brushed them gently until they were clean. In the earth that had been dug away from the ancient skeletons, however, the scientists noticed a piece of flint of the type used by Indians to make arrow and spear points. There it was in the loose soil. Where had it come from? Certainly it did not belong with the ancient skeletons, for everyone knew that all Bison taylorii had been long dead when the Indians first entered North America. But if it did not belong with the skele-

tons then how did it get down so deep in the earth?

The piece of flint was examined: it showed signs of having been chipped and flaked by human hands. It was actually a piece of a spearhead! Soon another piece of broken spearhead was turned up in the loose earth that had been removed from the bison skeletons. Now, the scientists grew very cautious—they were determined to find out where these bits of Indian weapons originated. All possible care was taken: every inch of bison bone was scrutinized as it was uncovered for more fragments of flint spear points or other tools.

The patient work paid off: as he was cleaning the thick, heavy ribs of a long-dead bison, one of the palaeontologists saw a bit of chipped flint protruding next to a rib. He carefully brushed away the dirt and saw a broken spear point wedged between the ancient ribs. The spear point fitted one of the fragments that had been discovered earlier, showing the diggers what the entire unbroken point must have looked like.

The discovery was amazing: the bison skeletons were found in the exact positions in which the animals had died; this meant they had never been disturbed. Sedimentation had covered them with gravel and clay, yet here was an Indian spearhead embedded between the ribs of a bison, as though the bison had been killed by an Indian hunter who had been wandering the plains of North America thousands of years ago.

Dr. J. D. Figgins, the director of the Colorado Museum, realized the importance of this discovery. He wanted to be able to show his fellow scientists exactly how the spear point lay in relation to the bison bone. So he had his assistants dig around the bones and the spear point, leaving the bones and spear point standing out on a raised block of earth. After coating the block with paper and plaster he lifted the entire mass out of the ground and transported it to the museum.

Most scientists still would not believe that Dr. Figgins' spear point had been driven between the bison ribs by an Indian hunter. They found it hard to believe that the Indians had inhabited our continent for such a long time, when they had been trained to think that the Indian civilizations could not be any older than two or three thousand years. They tried to show that the spear point was placed between the bison ribs naturally: by erosion, by a burrowing animal or in some way that did not involve Indian hunters.

Dr. Figgins was not to be dismayed: he returned to the Cimarron River for more excavations. Working among the bison skeletons, he quickly uncovered four more complete spear points, but each of them was disturbed in the process of excavation. The fifth spear point appeared, again between the ribs of a bison skeleton, and this time even greater care was taken. The point and the bone next to it were painstakingly uncovered, then telegrams were sent to prominent archaeologists to come and see the spear point *where it lay.* Several archaeologists came, they examined the skeleton, the clay and gravel beds above it, they looked at the point, they discussed and argued. Finally, the verdict was pronounced: the spear point had been thrust into the ribs of this bison by an ancient American Indian, more ancient than anyone had supposed an Indian could be. There was no chance that the spear point had got there by accident, said the archaeologists. We must now accept the fact that the American Indians were hunting on this continent long ago—as long ago as the end of the great Ice Age, when Bison taylorii was supposed to have lived.

Thus, anthropologists the world over came to change their opinions about the age of the American Indian race, all because of a flint spear point that had long ago reached its target deep in the side of a great bison.

More excavations went on at the Cimarron, and a total of fourteen spear points were recovered among the bison skeletons. The spear points were very unusual, not at all like the usual triangular stemmed points so often found. They were long and boat-shaped, with a groove running down each side, like those on bayonet blades. The scientists attached to these points the name of the nearby town, Folsom, and American archaeology had a new treasure: the Folsom point, whose makers were thereafter called Folsom Men.

Today many more archaeological sites of the Folsom Men have been discovered. They are all through the Western Plains, the Southwest and even along the East Coast, in Massachusetts, Pennsylvania, Maine and Virginia. From these excavations we know much more about the hunters who made the Folsom points. These people were true American Indians, who traveled in small bands of ten to fifteen perhaps, following huge tusked mammoths and bison that existed in North America after the Ice Age.

The Folsom Men had to live by hunting animals and gathering wild plant food, as no one in the world had yet discovered how to plant gardens or breed animals. They were constantly on the move, and when they camped, they built no houses, staying for only a few days at a time. Most Folsom sites are what the

archaeologists call "kill sites," places where the Folsom Men hunted down and killed a large mammoth or some bison, and butchered them to eat on the spot. After a few days, the hunters would depart, leaving the carcasses, a few broken stone scraping tools and knives, and a small campfire or two. Occasionally an ornament might be found, such as some notched-edge bone discs that were found in Colorado on the Lindenmeier Folsom camp site, named for its location on the Lindenmeier ranch. We even know something about how Folsom Men looked, thanks to a Texas cowboy, George McJunkin, who found a site with a fragmented Folsom period Indian skeleton. From this scientists have been able partially to reconstruct the appearance of the individual.

The new Carbon 14 time clock has given us the true age of the Folsom Men: ten thousand years ago. The maximum age of Indian habitation of the New World was originally believed to be two or three thousand years.

Now, as a result of more recent excavations in many early Indian sites, we know that the Folsom Men were *not* the first Indians to arrive here from Asia, but that they were descendants of even earlier immigrants who came across the Bering Straits more than fifteen thousand years ago.

Scientists no longer talk of the antiquity of the American Indian in terms of years or centuries but in terms of thousands of years before Christ. So profound is the effect of this sudden lengthening of our view into the past that a few archaeologists have indeed suggested that man might have reached the New World even earlier than the last glaciation of the Ice Age, an opinion that most people would have scarcely dared to hold before the discovery of Folsom Man.

# 5/ THE FOUNDATIONS OF CIVILIZATION

FOR HUNDREDS OF THOUSANDS of years, the men of the Old Stone Age, such as the Australopithecinae, the Neanderthals and the Folsom Indians, led a difficult and bleak existence that was basically the same. This was true despite the differences in climate in the various glacial periods, the differences caused by cultural evolution in which new tools and techniques were developed, and the different kinds of game and plant food available in the various areas of the world. The men of the Old Stone Age were hunters: in small bands they moved about over the endless expanse of the earth following the wild animals that provided them with most of their food.

Compare this Stone Age existence with the life in Egypt under the pharaohs. The Egyptians had a complicated nation of great size, ruled by a god-king who with the nobles and the priests was supported by a large lower class of laboring people. The Egyptians were great architects and engineers; they knew the secrets of building with colossal stones. In Egyptian society, metal workers, potters, sculptors and artists could be found in large numbers. Scribes were available to change the spoken word into marks on coarse papyrus paper. The Egyptians lived in large cities and villages, in permanent houses, farming the rich lands of the Nile Valley. From their fields came livestock, grain and other plant foods in great quantities, enough to support the farmers as well as the pharaohs and the nobles.

How did this great change take place? How were the footloose Stone Age hunters who roamed the world of the glaciers transformed into the city dwellers and farmers of ancient Egypt, Mesopotamia and China, who no longer hunted but remained tied to their homes, their gardens and their flocks? Truly a great change in the history of humanity took place when men left the hunt to settle down and farm. If this had not occurred, the way of life that we know today would be impossible. We would be wandering about on a perpetual hunt, living in crude shelters or caves.

Archaeologists have long hoped to find out more about this change in our way of life. When did it take place? Where did it take place? And *how* was it possible? For years, the periods leading up to the great civilizations of Egypt and Mesopotamia have been explored by archaeologists hoping to find the answers to these questions.

It was for this reason that an expedition from the

Oriental Institute of the University of Chicago ventured up into the hilly country of western Iraq in 1948, looking for evidence that would fill in the gap between the Old Stone Age hunters and the village dwellers of the later civilizations. The director of the expedition, Dr. Robert Braidwood, was hoping to find archaeological sites that would tell him how the ancient hunters had discovered how to raise wild animals in captivity and how they had learned to domesticate wheat and other grains for food. These two discoveries were the most important ever made in all of history, for they allowed man to stop wandering and settle down to a life of increased ease, with time to build better houses, make better tools and even to dream better dreams.

With these discoveries, the Old Stone Age ended and was replaced by the New Stone Age: the age of farmers and villages, upon which the civilizations of Egypt and Mesopotamia are built, and from which our own way of life is descended.

It was for a very special reason that Dr. Braidwood had picked the hills of Iraq for his search: according to studies made by botanists and zoologists, it was in this area that wild grasses were found from which wheat must have been domesticated. It was also in this area that various wild animal ancestors of the sheep and goat were found. Therefore, Braidwood reasoned, there was a good chance that the earliest domestication of plants and animals had actually been carried out in this region.

There was only one way to find out—go, see and dig! And this is what Dr. Braidwood and his staff were doing in 1948 in the hills of western Iraq, searching the ruins of ancient villages for the story of man's great step forward from food gatherer to food raiser.

In Iraq, foreign archaeologists cannot dig without the permission of the government. It is obtained through the Directorate General of Antiquities, which has a staff of trained Iraqi archaeologists. During Braidwood's explorations in 1948, these Iraqi archaeologists recommended that he examine a site located high on a steep-sided hill near the town of Kirkuk. The site appeared to be the remains of a very old settlement, so perhaps excavations there would reward Dr. Braidwood's efforts.

It was late in the season when he arrived at Jarmo, the lofty hilltop which his Iraqi colleagues thought was so interesting. For the non-archaeological visitor, there was little to distinguish this hilltop from others in the vicinity: it had the same grassy mantle, dotted here and there with stones and small shrubs. Only if one looked closely in the grass roots did one see the traces of ancient inhabitants of this spot—the abundant fragments of pottery and stone tools, and the vague outlines of low, practically buried, stone walls.

Excavations were begun to find out what kind of ruins lay beneath the surface of this grassy hilltop. As they dug carefully downward in their first test pits, the archaeologists discovered layer after layer of small ruined houses, discarded pottery fragments, stone knives, polished grinders, animal bones and the usual type of garbage that was bound to collect around an ancient village in the Near East.

All told, there were twelve layers, each layer representing a period during which the mud houses had gradually decayed to a point where they were beginning to be uninhabitable and were then rebuilt. They added up to about twenty-seven feet of accumulated archaeological deposits on the deserted hilltop.

The archaeologists realized that they had struck a truly important site, for the ruins of Jarmo contained a mixture of things which appeared to come from the Old Stone Age and things which were characteristic of the New Stone Age. For example, the stone knives found among the flimsy Jarmo houses were almost indistinguishable from those found in Old Stone Age sites, and these were found with the bones of *domestic* animals, a sign of the New Stone Age.

Dr. Braidwood returned three times more to his interesting little village in the hills of Kurdistan, and the peculiar features of the site which once appeared to be contradictory are now explained. Jarmo was one of the first real villages ever to be erected on the earth. It was built at a time when the way of life of the Old Stone Age was gone but not entirely forgotten. This was approximately nine thousand years ago, according to C 14 tests that have been done on charcoal from the deepest layers of the site. That is the reason why so many Old Stone Age tools appeared in the ruins, along with New Stone Age objects.

The earliest Jarmo was a village of small huts with mud walls built on stone foundations. The roofs of these huts were probably made of thatch or brush

of some sort. Each house consisted of several rectangular rooms, in one of which a fireplace or an oven was made in the clay floor. The archaeologists found faint traces of woven matting on the floors of these houses, matting made of rushes or plant fibers of some type.

The village was never very large, even at its greatest period. According to Dr. Braidwood it probably never consisted of more than twenty houses which could shelter perhaps 150 people at most. Still a permanent village of 150 was something that had never existed during 740,000 years of the Old Stone Age.

The mere fact that such a village could be built and kept up indicates that the people of Jarmo did not have to work as hard for their food as did their Stone Age ancestors. The Jarmo people had enough surplus food to permit them to take time off—time that could be used for building, art, trading or developing better tools.

The Jarmo dwellers would never have been able to build a village such as this if they had not known how to raise plants and animals. In the lowest layers of the site, tiny fragile remains of wheat and barley seeds were recovered by the careful excavators, and bones of domestic goats were also found. Bones of pigs, horses and cattle were also found, but it is difficult to say whether these were domesticated or not. Skeletons alone do not indicate this.

60

The religion of the Jarmo people must have been built around their farming activities, for there were many small animal figurines of unfired clay, all representing animals that were important for their food supply. Other figurines represent what Dr. Braidwood and his colleagues believe to be goddesses that controlled the bounty of the harvest.

Despite the fact that the people of early Jarmo knew how to model clay to produce little figures, they did not know how to make baked clay wares. In fact, it was only in the upper four layers of the Jarmo site that pottery appeared, indicating that the village had been in existence for some time before its invention.

Since pottery is generally found in New Stone Age archaeological remains, it is clear that the Neolithic farmers of early Jarmo were really quite "old-fashioned." Other things that also might be called "old-fashioned" were the chipped stone knives and drills. A close examination of the black obsidian of which many of these tools were made indicated that the Jarmo farmers had obtained it *through trade with other villages,* for no such obsidian is found within a radius of three hundred miles.

This is the earliest appearance of trade and commerce that was to become so important in the civilizations of the Near East, India, and China.

The signs of the great change in man's existence

were everywhere in the layered ruins of Jarmo. Stone-bladed sickles were found, showing the unmistakable high polish which was produced by the blades' being constantly swung against the nodding stalks of wheat and barley. Grindstones were found, some flat and rectangular with small rectangular hand stones, while others were deep and basin shaped. On these the wheat of Jarmo's gardeners had been ground, before being made into bread to be baked in the little bee-hive ovens in each house. These tools demonstrated that the Jarmo people had come to rely completely on agriculture and livestock for their existence. This

evidence was backed up by the remarkable absence of arrow and spear points and the other hunting weapons that are so often found in Palaeolithic excavations.

Although many of the stone tools had been made by chipping, like those of the Old Stone Age men, there were many tools that showed a completely new method of toolmaking—stone polishing. Beautifully polished stone adzes, balls, ornaments and weights were found in large numbers. Never before had such tools been produced: they were further evidence of the great changes that were taking place in the Kurdish hills that would someday affect all mankind.

The pyramids of Egypt and the gleaming temples of Greece are marvelous to see; they are monuments to mighty civilizations that have left their imprint upon our lives in very obvious fashion. But thanks to Dr. Braidwood's explorations, we have now come to see that the Egyptians, Greeks and the modern world, too, owe much to the events of nine thousand years ago in Kurdistan when lowly mud villages of farmers rose on hilltops. These ancient Iraqi farmers left the world a priceless treasure in their knowledge of the secrets of planting wheat and breeding animals. This treasure has been of more value to mankind than all the many treasures of Egypt and the Orient combined.

# 6/ THE SECRET OF CRETE

FROM THE BEGINNINGS of civilization, we now move to one of the great civilizations of the ancient Mediterranean. Here we deal with a piece of archaeological detective work that may never be surpassed.

In 1900, Sir Arthur Evans, a renowned British archaeologist, began excavations at a place called Knossos on the island of Crete, situated southeast of Greece in the Mediterranean, amid acres of ruins marking the site of an ancient settlement. According to the legends of the ancient Greeks, a great kingdom had built its capital at Knossos, and Evans had come to uncover remains of this forgotten, mysterious kingdom, known heretofore only from the vague words of the poets who lived in Greece long before the birth of Christ.

The promise of the old legends was more than fulfilled by what Evans found, for Knossos turned out to have been the capital of what we now know as the Minoan Civilization, an empire of sea rovers who held sway over much of the eastern Mediterranean Sea between 1900 B.C. and 1650 B.C. Evans uncovered the huge palace of the Minoan sea kings, a building

65

with many-storied halls, decorated with beautiful murals of sea animals, warriors, lovely women and acrobats cavorting with bulls. This great palace contained a complete system of running water that supplied numerous inside bathtubs, much like our own. Deep in the palace's maze of halls and corridors were storerooms containing quantities of olive oil, grain, tools, furniture and implements—all that was necessary to support the royal family and the army of servants who attended to their needs.

In the graves about the palace were the remains of the Minoan rulers, laden with gold and precious stones, often watched over by the strange snake goddess who played such an important part in the Minoan

religion. The palace also contained a kind of library or record room, in which quantities of clay tablets had been kept. These tablets were inscribed with characters in a completely unknown hieroglyphic writing system. Because these tablets had been made of unbaked clay, they would have been completely destroyed by time if this great palace had not been ruined by either invasion or an earthquake. A fire had followed, and the little clay tablets had been baked in the flames and preserved for Evans's spade in 1900.

Evans tried to decipher the characters on the tablets but could do very little. He recognized three different kinds of writing on the tablets. Two of these were represented on only a few tablets, but the other, which

Evans called "Linear B" (because it was written in lines), existed in large quantities. Evans set to work on Linear B but he managed to identify only some simple signs as numbers. He was certain, however, that the language of the characters was not Greek, because the archaeological remains with which he found the tablets were so different from those found on mainland Greece.

For many years, Evans's work on Crete continued. He brought more and more to light about the brilliant civilization of the Minoans, but the riddle of the Minoan hieroglyphs remained unsolved. Although many archaeologists and linguists worked diligently to find the key to the scratchings on the clay tablets, no one succeeded.

Late in his career, Evans gave a lecture on the Minoan civilization to a group of schoolchildren visiting the British Museum and told them of the strange hieroglyphs and the difficulties that archaeologists were facing with them. Among these students was a boy named Michael Ventris, whose interest and imagination were kindled by the story of this ancient mystery, and he resolved to do something about the problem himself.

Young Ventris learned Egyptian hieroglyphs at an early age, and threw himself wholeheartedly into the study of Latin and Greek. His enthusiasm for the

Minoan hieroglyphs never lapsed even when he rode a British bombing plane as a navigator during World War II, or after the war, when he studied architecture, which became his profession.

During the years that Ventris was studying and fighting in the war, further studies were being made on the Minoan tablets, and some facts about the Linear B script had been uncovered. Certain signs had been identified as standing for "man," others as meaning "woman." Other signs indicated grammatical endings like "ing" or "s" in English.

It was further known that the hieroglyphs were of two types: syllabic (standing for syllables like "sis" and "bin") and ideographic (representing ideas or things like "man," "water" or "boat"). It was possible to deduce this because there were too many symbols for the system to be purely alphabetic, as our writing system is, and yet there were too few signs for the system to be ideographic like Chinese. The meanings of some signs, however, such as "man" and "woman," were known to be ideographic. Therefore, the system was a combination of ideographic and syllabic signs.

Deciphering an unknown writing in an unknown language is extremely difficult. Intelligence agents have developed many techniques for breaking secret codes which are just like unknown writing systems.

However, a coded message from a Russian spy, for example, will decode into the Russian language. How do you start if you do not know what language your message will decode to, and how do you go about it if the language may be a completely lost one spoken several thousand years ago?

Ventris was not dismayed by this challenge. After World War II he began to work on the Linear B clay tablets in earnest, obtaining copies of all the inscriptions on every tablet that had been excavated on Crete and on the mainland of Greece.

How Ventris conducted his exploration of the Minoan script shows what can be done to decipher a written language without knowing actually what the language is. In a long and tedious period of study and comparison of the tablets, he worked out the system of signs used. Minoan writers had different handwriting, just as you or I, and it was necessary to know which were merely personal variations of signs, and which were actually different. Then Ventris identified certain words by noting combinations of signs that reappeared on tablet after tablet. In some cases, he was able to identify more kinds of grammatical endings that were attached to these words. In other cases, he could actually tell that some words were nouns and others were verbs, for example, or conjunctions. Nouns

were simple to identify: some tablets looked like lists of items; they consisted of sequences of number signs and other kinds of signs. Clearly, the numbers stood for quantities and the signs next to them told the kinds of things that were counted. In addition, nouns seemed to have certain kinds of grammatical endings, different from the endings of other words.

Then Ventris accomplished a truly great feat. Without any more knowledge of the Minoan language than any other archaeologist, he was able to work out the syllable system and discover the number of vowels in the language as well as the number of consonants. He did this by carefully comparing all the different grammatical word endings, especially those of words thought to be nouns.

He discerned patterns in the noun endings: some patterns appeared to indicate differences in number, others in gender. By making shrewd guesses based on other ancient Mediterranean languages, and checking these by trial substitutions, he was finally able to determine for each syllable the vowels and consonants used.

But the actual sounds represented by these syllable signs eluded him. The great Sir Arthur Evans, Ventris's source of inspiration, had stated definitely that the language of the Minoans was *not* Greek. Ventris had followed this lead and looked for connections between the Minoan script and the language of the Etruscans, a group who inhabited Italy before the rise of the Roman Empire.

Try as he would, Ventris simply could not make sense of the script by substituting Etruscan sounds for the strange hieroglyphs. Finally, almost in desperation, he tried to fit the syllable system of the Minoan script to the ancient Greek language. Some words suddenly became translatable when he tried substituting Greek sounds for the Minoan signs. Others, however, appeared to be as far from decipherment as ever. However, he pushed on, trying with all his knowledge and powers of reasoning to see if the connection between Greek and Minoan had not escaped him. Gradually the truth dawned: the Minoan hieroglyphs actually represented Greek, *but not the Greek to which Ventris had tried to translate them.* Minoan Greek, it appeared, was considerably different from the Greek that Ventris had used: Minoan Greek should have been—it was eight centuries older!

Once this was realized, the vowels and consonants of the syllable signs were identified rapidly, the meanings of the ideographs were soon unraveled, and Ventris was able to read the strange script on the dusty little tablets. He gradually compiled a dictionary of Minoan words and grammatical endings which could be used by archaeologists as they found other tablets in Minoan ruins in Crete. As the mystery of the tablets faded away, new facts sprang up in its place, facts that told of a completely unknown side of the Minoan civilization, recorded by the hands of long-dead scribes in the great sea king's palace at Knossos.

The tablets turned out to be palace records of events that had occurred before the palace had burned down. The tablets themselves were probably only "carbon copies" of other documents that had been written on skins or papyrus paper and had perished in the fire and destruction of the palace. These "carbon copies" were evidently kept in the palace record rooms, filed in labeled baskets and boxes, for a year or so, and then destroyed. They were seldom kept long, for they contain *no dates,* which are necessary for long-term record keeping.

With the aid of the tablets we can see that the Minoans were far more like us than the ruins of their beautiful palaces and tombs made them seem. We find the roll call of a chariot squadron, listing the charioteers, their armor and equipment. We also find lists of "drafted" rowers, probably destined to serve on the fleet Minoan galleys. The lists often contain notes that certain rowers failed to report for duty. There are tax lists, showing that not all Minoans had to pay regular taxes: the smiths who made the bronze weapons of war, for example, were excused from them. Others

simply did not pay their taxes. We can only wonder what happened to them.

Kings, priests, generals and royalty are often mentioned, and from these clay records we know more now about the Minoan government. It is clear that beneath the kings were a group of nobles of lesser rank, each of whom held large tracts of land, administering them for the king. On these lands were villages which were presided over by a minor official. There seems to have been a supreme commander of military forces, called the Leader of the Host, who exercised considerable authority. Just as we have warning systems to defend our country against attack, so the Minoans had permanent coastal lookouts who would sound the alarm when enemy ships appeared.

Other tablets speak plainly of the fact that the Minoans traded for and used large numbers of slaves, evidently captured in Asia Minor or in other coastal regions of the Mediterranean.

The Minoans planted wheat fields, for which they were assessed taxes. They also raised cattle, pigs and sheep, and used dogs for hunting. One tablet gives a list of oxen with names such as Blondie, Bawler and Whitefoot. Evidently Minoans had a sense of humor!

Before long, Ventris had progressed so far in his work with Minoan that he and his associates were able to write to each other in Minoan script. The archaeologists of the world applauded the work of the quiet but brilliant young architect and justly so: he had accomplished the most difficult decipherment job that the world has even seen. His work was far more difficult than that of Champollion, the famous French scholar who finally broke the Egyptian hieroglyphs. Champollion knew that the hieroglyphs stood for Egyptian sounds; furthermore he had the Rosetta Stone, upon which an Egyptian inscription had been written with a *Greek translation.*

Thus the brilliant and gifted Michael Ventris, by his skillful painstaking analysis and comparison, cracked the puzzle of sixty years of Cretan archaeology. At the age of twenty-seven, he stood at a pinnacle of success, far above archaeologists who had spent a lifetime digging in the Mediterranean. Yet he was not fated to make more outstanding contributions. He died in an auto accident in 1956. His genius was rare, and he was one of those that the world will truly miss, but he left behind a monument that cannot be overlooked.

# 7/ THE DEAD SEA SCROLLS

FOR THOSE who would emulate Michael Ventris, be forewarned: there are only two major untranslated scripts in the world—the Indus Valley and Maya Indian scripts.

The Indus Valley script consists of a large number of hieroglyphic signs appearing in very short inscriptions on small rectangular stamp seals that were used to mark soft fabrics. The shortness of the inscriptions and the probability that they are personal names and titles make it difficult to attack them in the manner used by Ventris on Linear B. The Mayan Indian script has been partially deciphered: calendar dates, numbers, month names, etc. can be read and some titles on monuments have been tentatively identified. The key to Mayan hieroglyphics once existed in the form of many crude books, but these were burned as works of the Devil by the Spanish conquistadores and the knowledge died with the Indian priests who knew the script. The task of deciphering Mayan hieroglyphs will be nearly as difficult as that of the Indus script because the inscriptions are generally very short.

As the supply is short, speed is necessary, for soon

79

undeciphered scripts may cease to exist. This will really not be serious, however, for there is still much to be done with the known written languages of the ancient world, and there is every indication that Sumerian, Akkadian, Assyrian, Egyptian, Etruscan and Hebrew inscriptions and documents still contain surprises. One of these surprises is, in fact, the subject of this chapter —a discovery of great significance for two of the world's great religions.

In A.D. 70 the gleaming white buildings of the little monastery perched on the hilltop of Qumran, high above the Dead Sea in Palestine, echoed to the sounds of frantic activity. Every day for years the religious people who lived there had gone about their quiet, well-ordered lives, praying, meditating, copying sacred books for their library and performing the work that had to be done to provide the group with food and clothing. Throughout the years, the only sounds that had broken the routine of daily living for the holy hermits had been the little bells that signaled the start of each new day, telling them when to work and pray; the muffled footsteps and lowered voices of the brethren as they moved about at their tasks; and the low monotone of the master dictating to the scribes.

Now, however, the hermits hurried to and fro in a bedlam of noise. The reason was clear: the Jewish revolt against the rule of the Romans had failed. The

Jews were split by quarrels among themselves and could not unite to face the advancing legions of Rome, under the Roman general Vespasian; his eagles and standards were gradually reoccupying the disputed areas of the Holy Land from which they had been driven a few years earlier. Israel had lost all hope of overthrowing its conquerors. Now they were to pay the price of rebellion in blood and lives taken by the short-bladed swords and long javelins of the Roman

soldiers. Jerusalem was already in flames; even the great temple of Solomon was destroyed.

The people in the little monastery knew that it soon would be their turn to fall beneath the Roman onslaught. Their first and only thoughts were for their books—the collection of sacred scrolls that had grown in their library through the years, carefully copied by patient scribes who sat all day long bent over their work tables, quills in hands. To the religious people of the monastery, these scrolls mattered more than life itself, for they contained the knowledge and prophecies of the holiest of men. The hermits would die, but the word of God must be preserved.

And so they set to work, lifting the scrolls from the simple library shelves, wrapping them tightly, and placing them in tall, narrow jars, upon which tops were fitted. As the jars were filled and sealed, they were carried down from the monastery hill with loving care into the gleaming heat of the parched valley of the Dead Sea. In the cliffs that surrounded the valley of the sea, certain caves were known to exist. These caves would surely be shelter for the precious books. The Romans would not think of looking in that desolate region for these well-hidden caves.

The hermits worked rapidly, for they did not know how soon the columns and squares of the Roman legions would appear on the horizon. Then they would no longer be able to hide their "treasury of the spirit." The job was soon done. The jars were neatly lined up on the cave floors so they could be easily identified when and if the hermits returned to claim them.

The seasons passed; the years rolled by, and the tall brown jars stood straight in their hiding places like soldiers on some eternal guard post, waiting for the hermits to return. But they never did, for the monastery was in ruins and its inhabitants scattered to the four winds by the avenging Romans.

The years turned to centuries and the centuries slipped away, and still the jars stood in the gathering dust, visited only by the jackals, snakes and lizards of this arid land. It was not until 1,877 years had passed that their charmed repose was broken.

Then, as so often happens in archaeology, it was not a scientist who first set eyes upon the heritage of the monastery of Qumran. It was the tanned, lean Bedouins of the Ta'amire tribe, who were skulking about in the Dead Sea region, trying to slip illegally between Jordan and Palestine. Those Bedouins were smugglers and could not afford to take the proper roads that normal travelers took. While detouring through the dry, rocky valley they tried to make the most of their lost time by searching the caves and ruins for ancient relics that might be sold to antique dealers in Palestine or Jordan for a handsome profit.

During the course of a careful search of the cliffs that rimmed the valley, a cave was discovered a short distance north of the hill upon which the monastery of Qumran had once stood. The cave had a small well-hidden entrance from which a passage led into a long, narrow chamber in which stood a quantity of the large jars.

The Bedouins never had seen anything like this before. What was in the jars—treasure? They lost no time in breaking open a few of the vessels to see what they contained. No doubt they were disappointed

when they found only rolls of shabby-looking material with writing on it. Having considerable knowledge of the local languages, the Bedouins decided that the writing was in a kind of script known as Syriac. These men were not sure about the value of these tattered rolls but they took them to Palestine in the hope of finding a buyer. Because the Bedouins believed that they were written in Syriac the scrolls were ultimately brought to the attention of the Metropolitan of the Syrian Orthodox Church, who directed a monastery in Jerusalem.

The Metropolitan saw immediately that the scrolls were not written in Syriac but in a form of ancient Hebrew script. He purchased some of the scrolls and attempted to have them identified by experts in the Hebrew language and literature. Many people called them worthless, but others came forward to present another view. The scrolls, they said, were very ancient, and were the greatest manuscript discovery of modern times, for there were almost no handwritten documents of greater age from the Holy Land. Interest rose even higher when it became clear that some of the scrolls were copies of books of the Bible. Here was a chance for the Bible scholars to see if their later Bible manuscripts were correct, by comparing them with the older manuscripts which the Bedouins had found.

While the Metropolitan bought some of the scrolls

found by the Bedouins, others were sold to different scholars and collectors. Word of the finds spread rapidly among archaeologists, Bible scholars and the Bedouins. Soon many institutions and scholars were attempting to obtain scrolls for research into this important period of history. Prices for the manuscripts rose greatly. A series of expeditions were sent to the area where the scrolls had been found. The Bedouins had been there first and had ransacked the cave where the original find had been made, turning everything upside down in their search for more scrolls. They turned up more scrolls elsewhere, but the scientific expeditions investigating twenty-five caves in the area also found several, including two scrolls of thin copper plate, impressed with the Hebrew characters.

While the search for new scrolls went on, those already found were being translated and analyzed by experts in ancient Hebrew, and by Biblical scholars. These men were trying to find out as much as they could from the scrolls themselves about the dates when they were written, who was responsible for the writing, and under what circumstances the scrolls were produced. In the caves along the Dead Sea, archaeologists were exploring and excavating to add to the evidence other scholars were obtaining in quiet laboratories where the scrolls were being unrolled and translated. Excavations were made at the ruins of the Qumran monastery which produced evidence that linked the inhabitants of the monastery to those who had hidden the scrolls so long ago in the caves.

Radiocarbon dating was done on samples of the scrolls and their wrappings. These tied in with the evidence of the pottery that contained the scrolls and coins found in the monastery ruins, showing indisputably that the scrolls and the monastery had existed well before Christ.

Today, research still goes on and scrolls are still being sought in the deserted land along the Dead Sea, but the archaeologists and the scholars, working hand in hand, have already given us a clear picture of the significance of the moldering scrolls.

These scrolls were the sacred books of a Jewish sect called the Essenes, who lived a quiet monastic life in the monastery of Qumran, during the years between 200 B.C. and A.D. 70. Although the scrolls were not hidden until A.D. 70, many were written in the two centuries before Christ and preserved in the monastery library until the coming of the Romans.

As some of the scrolls contain the rules of the monastery of Qumran, we know a great deal about the way the Essenes lived. Other scrolls are copies of books of the Old Testament, often with notes in the margin that display the ancient Essenes' thoughts about God, man and the world.

Most important and startling, however, was the find that greeted the translators when they began their work on some of the scrolls containing the writings of members of the Essene group. The words of the Essene hermits resembled those found in the *New* Testament, yet the scrolls were written in the two centuries *before the birth of Christ!* The ancient scrolls, ripped from their slumber of eighteen hundred years, have turned out to be a firm bridge between two of the world's greatest religions, Judaism and Christianity. Up to the discovery of the scrolls the only link between the two faiths had been Christ Himself, but the scrolls show that even before Christ men of wisdom were turning toward the ideals that Jesus Christ was later to teach. The philosophy of the Essenes was particularly strong in these ideals, and in this respect the Essenes differed from others of the Jewish faith. Thus, when Christ began His ministry, the Essene thought had already spread and laid a foundation for the acceptance of His teachings.

The words of the Essene hermits of Qumran, then, tell us of the period of wars and turmoil that saw the dispersion of the Jews and the rise of Christianity. They also have helped to forge a stronger link between the Jewish and Christian faiths, a link that should help the members of these two great religions to reach a better understanding of themselves and each other.

# 8/ THE SUNKEN GALLEY

THE PRECEDING CHAPTERS have dealt with the results of what archaeologists call "dirt archaeology"—excavating in archaeological sites, as opposed to collecting ancient stone tools, pottery, statues, etc., from the surface of the ground or studying visible ruins of buildings. The other chapters have also dealt with discoveries of great consequence for human history.

In this chapter, the discovery cannot rightfully be called dirt archaeology, for it was made beneath the sea, and the material which was discovered is not as important as the way in which it was discovered, for this discovery truly opens a whole new vista for archaeology.

At the laboratories of the Naval Undersea Research Group, in the sunny port city of Toulon, southern France, a life-and-death struggle was going on. Within the decompression chamber in the laboratories, a tough, grizzled Aqualung diver was fighting for his life. He had stayed too long in the blue-green world beneath the surface, had ventured too deep, and now his body was racked with the pain of the dreaded "bends" resulting from nitrogen bubbles that had formed in his blood vessels. He stood close to death's door. The tense doctors and scientists who had brought him from the sea twisted in agony were using all their knowledge to save him, trying to rid his blood stream of the deadly bubbles. The diver was a brave man; he hung grimly to life and with the help of the naval doctors began to climb the road to recovery. He lost all his toes, and his legs were so crippled that he could never dive again, but he would live.

During the long months of his recovery in 1951–52, the diver was often visited by one of his rescuers, an athletic young diver named Dumas, who was an assistant of the renowned inventor of the Aqualung, Jacques-Yves Cousteau. As the two divers exchanged stories about the world beneath the waves that they loved so well, they became good friends. One day, the crippled diver offered to tell his new friend all he knew about the sea around the port of Marseilles, where he had been salvage diving for years. Because he would never dive again the knowledge would do him no good, but perhaps Dumas would be interested. Dumas was, and he took down all that the older man had to say.

One point was particularly interesting. The diver was telling Dumas about his favorite lobster-hunting place, down the coast to the south of Marseilles in a barren, rocky area in the vicinity of four big rock islets rising from the sea. There, he said, by the island of

Grande Congloué, was a wonderful lobster ground. You went down along the face of the cliff and then just above the pots . . . "What pots?" asked Dumas, suddenly very much alert. "Oh, there are lots of pots down there on the bottom. They're long and narrow with pointed bottoms and two handles on the neck."

Dumas sketched an outline on his pad. "Like this?"

"Yes, that's it. Like that."

The outline that Dumas had sketched was of an ancient wine storage jar called an *amphora,* used by both Greeks and Romans. He had seen some in his diving around the Mediterranean, but had never heard of them in such quantity as the injured diver described them. This called for an investigation.

Within a few weeks, the Naval Undersea Research vessel *Calypso* put out from Marseilles with the usual crew of divers and undersea scientists aboard. Commander Cousteau accompanied Dumas, who had carefully obtained all the possible information on the "pots" off Grande Congloué from his convalescent friend. But one more person was aboard, a rather unusual man to be riding an undersea research vessel. He was Dr. François Benoit, Director of Antiquities of Provence and curator of the Marseilles Archaeological Museum.

Near the east side of the huge rock, the ship dropped anchor, and Cousteau and Dumas slid beneath the waves, clad in tight-fitting rubber suits for protection against the cold. Cousteau descended 220 feet down the steep face of the Grande Congloué rock, which was festooned with sponges and all sorts of sea animals. He reached the ocean floor and started back up. No amphorae were in sight. Had the diver given them bad directions? Suddenly, he saw a familiar shape half hidden in the silt of the ocean bottom. Was it? Yes, it *was* an amphora! He carefully lifted the big vessel from the muck of centuries and looked around for more—but there were none. Discouraged he stood the amphora upright and started toward the surface. Then, sixty feet above the first find he saw it—a huge area littered with amphorae and other kinds of pottery vessels. The air in his tanks was low and he had to surface, so he swooped over the litter of ancient pottery on the sea floor, grabbed three small dishes and a rusted metal hook, and started up.

He climbed the ladder to the *Calypso* and handed his prizes to the waiting Dr. Benoit, who recognized the dishes as a kind of pottery called Campanian ware that was made in Greece from the fourth to the second century B.C. These black, thin dishes were found in Greek sites all over the Mediterranean coast and had even been traded as far as Britain on the west and the Black Sea on the east.

There could be no doubt that what lay below at the

base of Grande Congloué was a wrecked galley from a period well before Christ, the oldest galley yet found beneath the Mediterranean. There was also no doubt that the galley was crammed with archaeological material and should be scientifically excavated. But how does one excavate a ruined ship buried in mud about 140 feet below the surface of the sea?

That problem was not so difficult as it might sound. Engineers built a big socketed concrete block high on the side of the island, above the wreck. From the socket a boom was extended, ladders were built so that men could scamper up and down the cliff face, and then a small shack was built on the concrete block near the boom. The shack held a pump that was used to draw up silt loosened by the divers in clearing the wreck. The silt was drawn up through a large hose hung from the boom. Later a second hose was added; water was pumped down through this at high pressure, so that the divers could use it to wash silt away from the wrecked ship without breaking the pottery.

Fifteen divers began work on the ship, going down into the cold depth in shifts. Because the ship was 140 feet deep it was possible to stay down for only seventeen minutes without going through decompression stages on the way up. One diver, a veteran frogman of the Indochina war, was killed during a deep dive, showing how dangerous the salvage really was.

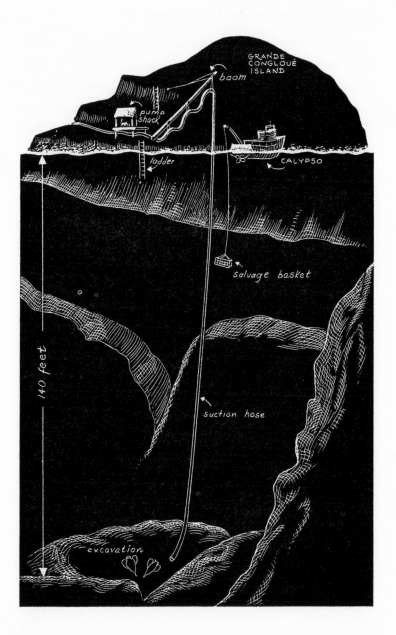

As the divers tried to clear away the covering of silt and expose the outlines of the ship itself, basket after basket of amphorae and other types of pottery found in the silt were filled and sent to the top. It soon became clear that the ship had sunk straight down to the bottom, where it was lying on a slanting rock shelf below the clifflike side of the island, the stern 140 feet below the surface, the bow about 112 feet deep.

The amphorae around the wreck came from a heavy load of these jars that had been stacked tightly on the lead-covered wooden deck of the ship. Part of this deck load was cleared away so that the underwater archaeologists could cut into the ship's hold. There they found more amphorae, shaped differently from those on the deck. And they found stacks and stacks of about forty different kinds of the black varnished Campanian ware that had first excited Dr. Benoit. The ship itself was very well made of pine, cedar and oak, held in place by long bronze nails and various iron fittings. To keep out marine worms, the hull had been covered with sheets of copper, and the decks were covered with lead sheets.

In the stern, lead piping was found, undoubtedly part of the lavatory for the ship's captain. Also on the stern were the remains of the crew's mess area, where Cousteau's men found pottery that had been used for cooking. It showed considerable wear.

High above the wreck, on a narrow rock shelf, was the huge crossbar of the ship's anchor where it had torn loose as the wreck sank down to Neptune's domain.

France was aflame with news of this amazing find. Cousteau and his hardy group of divers began to get more support for their work. The army, the Ministry of Education, the City Council, the Chamber of Commerce of Marseilles and the American National Geographic Society all helped. More archaeologists were added to the staff of the vessel. An underwater TV camera with a loud-speaker was developed so that archaeologists aboard the surface vessel could watch and direct the divers without even getting wet. Underwater six-thousand-watt flood lights were used to illuminate the scene so that the TV picture would be clearer.

As the never-ending train of pottery came over the side, archaeologists were overwhelmed. Never before had so much Campanian ware been found undamaged. Almost all that archaeologists knew of this pottery had been gleaned from broken pieces found in the rubbish heaps of Greek and Roman sites. Complete pots were rare. One Italian archaeologist had spent years on a study of the fragmentary Campanian ware from Italy and France only to see the pottery from the wreck at Grande Congloué make his work out of date.

Campanian ware had been actually factory-made in

Naples. Each pot bore the impression of the wooden molds with which it had been formed.

The main problem that the archaeologists had to solve concerned the ship itself: where was it from and how did it come to an end off Grande Congloué? It was a large vessel, probably completely sail-powered, without the rowers often used in Roman galleys. It could probably hold 10,000 jars the size of the amphorae or about 100,000 pounds of cargo.

Examination of the big amphorae revealed a seal on the neck of each one, a seal bearing the initials SES, followed by an anchor or a trident. This was probably the seal of the owner.

The archaeologists lost no time in tracing all available Roman family records. They found a number of references to one Marcus Sestius, who had been a wealthy merchant at approximately the period that the ship went down. This Sestius had been sent from Rome to the Greek Island of Delos to act in a dual capacity, first as a businessman, second as an espionage agent, acting to overthrow the Greek government there. Sestius had a trading business but nothing more was

found in the records, so a visit was paid to Delos itself. There a monument to Sestius was found, a monument raised to commemorate his receiving citizenship in the Greek community in 240 B.C.—a great honor for the Roman.

The hills of Delos are full of the ruins of the villas of ancient merchants and important people who inhabited that island. It was in the ruins of one of these villas that a solution was found to part of the mystery of the Grande Congloué ship. The ruin of a large spacious house displayed a beautiful mosaic floor in which were two designs, one showing Neptune's trident as an *E* with *S*'s in between the points, the other showing a dolphin, and a trident again oriented as an *E* flanked by two *S*'s. There was no doubt that this was Sestius' house. The mosaic designs were so close to those on the seals on the wine bottles that it was quite certain that the house and the sunken galley both belonged to the same man, the clever Roman merchant-spy, Marcus Sestius.

Now it remained to reconstruct the ship's passage and the cause of its destruction. The first load, placed

in the bottom of the hold, had been the amphorae filled with Greek wine. These had probably gone aboard in Delos. From Delos the ship had sailed westward across the Ionian Sea, thence between Sicily and the tip of Italy, and up the west coast. After a stop at Naples the hold was filled with boxes of black dishes, made in the pottery factories of the Neapolitans. After the pottery went aboard, the creaking deck was loaded with more amphorae. This time the wine came from the vineyards of Rome. The big galley rolled out into the sea and up the Italian coast, pushing toward Marseilles, called Marsalia by the Romans.

Then the crew began to tap the wine jars, as is shown by the small holes drilled in the sides of many jars. Perhaps the crew became too merry, for one black night, close to Marsalia, the ship drifted in close to what is now Grande Congloué, smashed its hull and sank quickly. The sobered sailors had a long, cold swim to shore through shark-infested waters, while the ship nestled down for its 2,200-year sleep.

Commander Cousteau and his men have opened up a whole new vista for the world with their pioneering of the marvelous Aqualung invention. They have also done archaeology a great service, for they have developed techniques for working in an environment that archaeologists had never entered. Their work on old Marcus Sestius' galley is a milestone, marking the use

of TV cameras, suction and pressure hoses, underwater flood lights and loudspeakers. All the engineer-
ing tasks that went into this job are examples for the
archaeological world to follow.

Aqualung archaeologists have since located the
wrecks of many more Roman galleys about the Mediterranean; and, in the sacred wells of the Maya cities
in Yucatan, Aqualungers are bringing up the remains
of sacrifices thrown long ago for the appeasement of
the gods. Off the coast of Florida, a huge sinkhole used
as a burial ground by Palaeo-Indians ten thousand
years ago has also been discovered and scientifically
explored. Cousteau has shown the way, and others are
not lagging behind.

# CONCLUSION

WE HAVE REACHED the end of this account of some of the great archaeological discoveries of recent years. Two main impressions that I hope I have been able to impart to the reader deserve restating here.

It should be very clear that great archaeological discoveries were not only made in the past, but are being made *now* and will continue to be made in years to come. The frozen tundra of the Arctic Circle, the glaring deserts of Afghanistan, the teeming tropical forests of Asia, Africa and America and the beautiful Pacific islands all hold the keys to many as yet unlearned secrets of the past of the human race. Each year brings new information about some part of man's past, and old theories are revised or thrown out to make way for the new facts, which themselves will someday have to make way for further discoveries. The archaeological horizons today are wider than ever before; armed with the best techniques of modern science, archaeologists are digging into the past in all areas of the world, filling in, bit by bit, the vast unknowns of human history.

What good does it do to reconstruct the lives of ancient peoples? They are gone—what good can this do?

It can do much good, actually, if we let it. Archaeology is just an extension of history, sociology (the study of social organization) and ethnology (the study of the cultures of living human societies). Archaeology takes up where these sciences stop, at the point were written historical records no longer exist. Together with history and sociology and ethnology, archaeology helps us to understand better what is happening now, by telling us what happened in the *deep past*. History picks up the story in the more recent past, and ethnology and sociology carry it on today. And so, archaeology is a very practical science; it can help us in guiding our national policy as much as historical studies can. It can tell us the long-hidden reasons for many things happening now and show us the beginnings of many great changes still going on in human society. With archaeology we can better understand why nations of people are as they are, and how our own present way of life came about.

Thus, archaeology is by no means either a dead science or a useless one, and the promise of the future for archaeologists and would-be archaeologists is as bright as the past has ever been. To those who may make the great discoveries about which some future volume may be written I should like to offer my best wishes for good digging.

# Suggestions for Further Reading

The list of books below is for the reader who wishes to find out more about the archaeological discoveries discussed in this book and other discoveries of recent times. Many of the books listed are of an advanced nature: this is because in many cases recent archaeological discoveries have not yet been presented in popular books.

Some of the books recommended here will also be found on reading lists dealing with other archaeological topics. They are included on this list because they contain information on *recent* discoveries, regardless of what other information they contain.

## GENERAL

WHEELER, SIR MORTIMER. *Archaeology from the Earth.* New York: Oxford University Press, 1954.
A comprehensive guide for those who wish to know the "how" and "why" of modern archaeology by a pioneer in archaeological techniques.

WHEELER, SIR MORTIMER. *Still Digging.* London: Pan Books, Ltd., 1958.

The autobiography of a colorful and brilliant modern archaeologist.

## EGYPT

GONEIM, M. ZAKARIA. *The Lost Pyramid.* New York: Rinehart & Co., Inc., 1956.

An Egyptian Egyptologist tells the story of the discovery of a "new" pyramid 4,500 years old.

## THE MAYAS

THOMPSON, J. E. S. *The Rise and Fall of Mayan Civilization.* Norman, Okla.: The University of Oklahoma Press, 1954.

A most readable up-to-date picture of the ancient Mayans and their way of life, by an expert in the field.

## THE MINOAN CIVILIZATION

CHADWICK, JOHN. *The Decipherment of Linear B.* New York: Modern Library Paperback, Random House, 1958.

An assistant of Michael Ventris tells the story of the exciting quest for the key to Linear B.

## THE NEAR EAST

BRAIDWOOD, LINDA. *Digging Beyond the Tigris*. New York: Schuman, 1953.

An account of the Oriental Institute Expeditions to Iraq (in the course of which Jarmo and other new sites were discovered), with some emphasis on methods of excavation.

BURROWS, MILLAR. *The Dead Sea Scrolls*. New York: The Viking Press, 1955.

The history of the scrolls and a consideration of their interpretations.

DAVIES, A. POWELL. *The Meaning of the Dead Sea Scrolls*. New York: Mentor Books, New American Library, 1956.

A modern scholar tells of the discovery of the scrolls, the scientific methods employed to authenticate and date them, and the controversies involving them.

GLUECK, NELSON. *Rivers in the Desert*. New York: Farrar, Straus & Cudahy, 1959.

Glueck, an expert on the archaeology of the Holy Land, tells of his recent work in Israel's Negev Desert, once an important link between three continents.

## NORTH AMERICA

LEWIS, T. M. N., and MADELINE KNEBERG. *Tribes That Slumber: Indian Tribes in the Tennessee Region*. Knoxville, Tennessee: University of Tennessee Press, 1958. An attractively illustrated, well-written volume on the life of the ancient Tennessee Indians, based on the archaeology of the region, much of which has been done in recent years.

MARTIN, PAUL S. *Digging into History.* Chicago Natural History Museum, Popular Series, Anthropology, No. 38, 1959.

An account of one of the prehistoric cultures of the Southwestern U.S., the Mogollon culture. As well as giving a clear picture of early Indian life, this volume tells much about archaeological methods.

WORMINGTON, H. M. *Ancient Man in North America.* Denver Museum of Natural History, Popular Series No. 4, 4th edition; fully revised 1957. Denver: Peerless Printing Company.

A detailed but very readable volume on Palaeo-Indian finds, containing chapters on Ice Age geology, dating techniques and individual Palaeo-Indian sites throughout the U.S.


## PALAEOLITHIC ARCHAEOLOGY

BRAIDWOOD, ROBERT J. *Prehistoric Men.* Chicago Natural History Museum, Popular Series, Anthropology Number 37; 3rd edition, 1957.

A handy, well-written outline of the prehistory of Europe and the Near East from the Old Stone Age to the dawn of civilization. Descriptions of Jarmo and related sites are included.

Coon, C. S. *The Seven Caves*. New York: Alfred Knopf, 1957.

Coon tells of his own excavations in untouched Stone Age caves of the Mediterranean and Near East, while presenting at the same time some interesting stories of the modern inhabitants of these regions.

Dart, Raymond, with D. Craig. *Adventures with the Missing Link*. New York: Harper & Brothers, 1959.

An account of Australopithecus finds up to the discovery of Olduvai Gorge.

Oakley, Kenneth P. *Man the Tool Maker*. Chicago: University of Chicago Press, 1957.

An excellent beginners' guide to the Old Stone Age cultures, giving information on recent discoveries in all parts of the world.

## PERU

Mason, J. Alden. *The Ancient Civilizations of Peru*. London: Pelican Books, 1957.

A summary of Peruvian prehistory as revealed by very recent archaeological excavations and a discussion of the great Inca empire.

## POLYNESIA

MÉTRAUX, ALFRED. *Easter Island: A Stone Age Civilization of the Pacific.* New York: Oxford University Press, 1957.

A famous ethnologist discusses the Easter Islanders, their way of life and their past, based on his expedition to that island in 1936.

SUGGS, R. C. *The Island Civilizations of Polynesia.* New York: Mentor Books, Ancient Civilizations Series, New American Library, 1959.

A timely account of the prehistory of the Polynesians, incorporating accounts of hitherto unpublished archaeological discoveries in the islands of Polynesia.

## UNDERWATER ARCHAEOLOGY

COUSTEAU, JACQUES-YVES, with FRÉDÉRIC DUMAS. *The Silent World.* New York: Harper & Brothers, 1953.

Cousteau's underwater adventures, including his archaeological explorations.

# Index

# About the Author

*Robert C. Suggs has recently conducted archaeological and anthropological explorations in the Marquesas Islands and French Polynesia. He has also engaged in anthropological research in Tahiti and Fiji. In the United States, he has undertaken field studies at Southern Connecticut Indian sites and colonial American locations in New York.*

*As Associate Anthropologist with Dunlap and Associates, Inc., a research and consulting firm, Dr. Suggs's work centers on social and psychological difficulties of the men who will operate advanced weapons systems and on the problems of civil defense.*

*Born in Portchester, New York, Dr. Suggs studied anthropology at Columbia University where he received his Ph.D. degree in 1959. He lives in Bridgeport, Connecticut, with his wife and son.*

# About the Illustrator

*Leonard Everett Fisher received his early training at the Art Students League, at the studio of Moses and Raphael Soyer and at the Hecksher Foundation in New York City. He received both a B.F.A. and an M.F.A. from the Yale University School of Fine Arts.*

*He interrupted his studies during World War II to serve in the army as a topographic editor and a photogrammetrist (making maps from photographs). Mr. Fisher, who has illustrated more than seventy books (and is the author of three), has served as Dean of the Whitney School of Art in New Haven, Connecticut.*

*Mr. Fisher, his wife and three children live in Westport, Connecticut.*